Staring Down the Tracks

Julia Paul

A Publication of The Poetry Box®

Poems ©2020 Julia Paul
All rights reserved.

Editing & Book Design by Shawn Aveningo Sanders.
Cover Design by Shawn Aveningo Sanders.
Cover Photograph by Robert R. Sanders.

No part of this book may be reproduced in any manner whatsoever without permission from the author, except in the case of brief quotations embodied in critical essays, reviews and articles.

ISBN: 978-1-948461-48-1
Printed in the United States of America.
Wholesale Distribution via Ingram.

Published by The Poetry Box®, 2020
Portland, Oregon
ThePoetryBox.com

For Brendan

From Darkness to Light

11/28/1982 – 1/18/2020

In the United States, in 2017 alone, 197 people died every day from drug overdoses. The numbers have not significantly changed since, despite increasing awareness of the epidemic that holds massive numbers of individuals in its chokehold. The statistics, startling as they are, fail to include countless others who suffer or die from conditions related to addiction, such as homelessness, poverty, infections and chronic illnesses. This is a wildfire burning everywhere. It should be impossible to turn away from those who struggle with this disease, just as we don't turn away from victims of other diseases and disasters, but the stigma surrounding addiction encourages the false and dangerous notion that addiction is a choice and a character defect. As a society, we haven't yet learned how to look into the eyes of the person holding a cardboard sign at the highway underpass.

Contents

Tracks	7
Black Dot	8
Nowhere	9
Broken Flesh	10
Denial	11
Say It Like You Mean It	12
The Addict's Mother	13
Distance	14
Remembering Jessica McClure	15
Wake and Watch	16
Just Coffee and Dessert	17
Holding the Pin Between Her Teeth	18
He Said	20
Francesca and Sonia	22
At Memorial Hospital	23
Spell for Detatching	24
At the Corner of Broad and Chance	25
This Poem	26
Delivering Thanksgiving Dinner Under the Bridge	27
Broken Boy: The Fractured Tale	28
The Summer of Fire	30
Christmas Visit	31
Ritual	32
One Summer Day	33
Recovery Prayer	34
Acknowledgments	37
Praise for *Staring Down the Tracks*	39
About the Author	41
About The Poetry Box®	43

Tracks

Clothespin-thin, he lugs bundles
    of belongings down a dirt path
        to a canopy of trestles over the old tracks
            behind Sav-A-Lot and Soapy Suds.

Homeless is the turn of a knob   a door opening
to a spot in the woods   where rivulets of mud
                follow the tracks.

Holes in his shoes.
    Holes in his tent pull the cold rain through.
Nothing's whole.

            Sean and Sharon
        see him begging
            for money outside Walmart.
                Don't recognize him,
so skinny and with dreads now.
        They lock the car doors.
            Hey Sharon,
                he says to the glass.

He roots through what's left at the curbs,
    couches and mirrors and crock pots.
            This and that a barter for survival.

He makes deals
    with the dealer
        who deals
            out of the bodega on King Street.
Grandmothers look the other way,
            bundles clutched tight.

        He finds no vein for happy.
Just to be touched,
      he wraps his arms   across his chest.

Black Dot

This is what loneliness looks like,
defined by what surrounds it.
A single black balloon
slipping through white sky.

This is the period sitting stone-still
at the end of a sentence,
any sentence, including this one.

This is what God looks like
from behind closed eyes,
faceless and distant.

This is the soul
according to some.
The soul, blackened by sin,
the light of grace snuffed out.

No.

This is the needle mark.
This is the black hole
into which the self disappears.
This is the exit wound.

Nowhere

He leans against a plank of light
        discarded by the sun, lies in blankets

of snowfall, showers in the rain. Wind
        whips his flesh dry. Concrete

slaps his soles. He's out in the open
        where all exit signs point. Night

is a dark cathedral padlocked by the moon.
        When New England weather

becomes mean as the shopkeeper
        who chases him from the sidewalk,

that bridge becomes roof. Others gather
        there, too. Like a borrowed library book,

such refuge can't be owned. He's got a spot.
        A spot is respected, is sacred, is everything.

Broken Flesh

Among the wandering and lingering
on this street of boarded-up bodegas

and discarded nips, a young man
descends Broad near Madison.

Long strawberry blond hair
tags him not from this neighborhood.

Not lost, though, he stops to chat
with that trio of men he knows.

Closer now, his face broadcasts
the distinct scabs of an addict.

He gestures with a hand pocked
with track marks, some fresh,

still glistening, almost pretty,
like dew caught by sunlight.

Somewhere else, his mother clutches
a coffee cup as morning stabs

through her window blinds.
Notice the remnants of a manicure,

still glossy but chipping, chipping.
Notice also her palms. How their lines

arc and tangle like tree branches
felled by a storm. And her face, trace

its map to the heart that beats
like a fist against a locked door.

Denial

Because only 59% of the moon's surface
       is visible from Earth,
            because we don't see the dirt
in the water until it rings the tub
or the dust until we move
            the sofa from the wall,

it's possible to pretend
       from heaven we don't appear
            as dirt and dust or shadow
even before the weeping
       in the graveyard begins.

            It's possible to sit under the stars
       and pretend they're beautiful
and that their beauty is not
            derived from the violence of the cosmos,
       that the cosmos is not
at war with itself.

            We see the stars thousands of years
       after they're dead. The sky's
a cemetery of ghosts, yet we lift
            our eyes to that light.

            Lake mirrors sky's tiny flames.
Moonlight floats on dual surfaces.
       It's possible to be blind
            to the dark side of the moon,
the pocked face turned toward Heaven,
       forehead pressed against that closed door.

Say It Like You Mean It

Say consequence.
Say it like it's a plastic bag
stuck on a tree limb, limp
until a breath of breeze.
Say consequence as it lifts and circles.
Say consequence to the fish out of water,
to anything that can't exist in the wind forever.

With fire on your breath, say consequence,
like a candle licking the curtain's hem.
Say consequence to the dead
for whom the votive glows red
in the dark cathedral of memory.
Say it like it's the rain that floods
the broken-down shack of your heart,
where behind a boarded-up window
a sad drunk puts on lipstick called *In the Pink*.

Say consequence is a rock through a window,
a suicide bomber, a shunned lover.
Say consequence to the man on the rooftop after
the flood, to the junkie in the all-night laundromat.
Say it with your boots.
Say it to a man with his neck in the noose.

End every sentence with consequence.
Say consequence is the penance.
Say it again and again, insistent
as sin. Say it like you mean it,
not like the French say it, soft as caramel.
Say it from the back of your throat.
Say it like knives into flesh,
like a needle aimed for a vein.

The Addict's Mother

                knows this snow
is beautiful. Lace
        filigrees the bark
of a slim maple
           while the sun
glitters the ground.
           She could cry
for all that is soft.
           So soft.
To look out
           and see nothing
but white,
           as though the world
has disappeared.
           Beyond the spinning
and lifting veils
           of squalling snow
a bus travels
           the turnpike,
its single passenger
           adrift.

Distance

How to calculate the miles we stumble
blindfold down the dark hallway?

We measure our grief against our neighbor's.
Lean on those yardsticks like crutches.

On the door's edge, lines marking height.
This child inches his way up. Initials and dates

with black Sharpie. This child of the rulers
walks countless steps to infinity.

How to measure the distance between
I will and I won't, I do and I don't?

How to measure our silences?
Not in the empty room. Not there. Here,

at the table of drifting voices. Those silences,
to hear, one's ear must be tuned to.

Not the rustle of leaves. What wind
carries within: the silence of clouds.

There are things that can't be calculated.
Where, he asked, *does the air end?*

How could she tell him it depends
on who's gasping and why.

Remembering Jessica McClure

With the money she gives him to buy
Christmas presents for others,
he purchases pencils at the Dollar Store
that say:
    I'm Addicted / to Sudoku
but he's not,
he's addicted to heroin
    for which there are no pencils
    or balloons or key chains
    on spinning racks   just drops
of blood that stain T-shirts
and wax wrappers in the dryer's lint catcher,
dozens of them   and the hole
into which he's slipped
like little Jessica who fell into an abandoned well
and landed so far down that rescuers
had to dig a parallel shaft and tunnel over
at an angle until they reached her
fifty-eight hours later when they heard
her singing, *Winnie the Pooh,*
    Winnie the Pooh.
    Tubby little chubby,
    all stuffed with fluff,
    he's Winnie the Pooh,
except from the depths of what has swallowed
her son comes only the sound of coins
tossed into his begging cup.

Wake and Watch

Wake
is parting waters,
is aftermath,
is tomorrow.

Sun
is chewed fingernail,
ragged under torn sky,
is tinder and cinder.

The heat
of the day is not begun,
is building muscle.

The heart
is muscle,
auto-rhythmic
in its blossoming grief.

Pine
is tower of boughs,
is state of the heart,
is box.

The watch
is only begun.
The watch
is tick-less, wait-less.

The heart
is watcher at the well.
Coins tossed
into bottomless waters.
Wake left by wishes.

The heart
begs for change.

Just Coffee and Dessert

She's advised to have spinach pie
and Greek salad at Frankie's Diner,
down the hill from the detox center,
while she waits to see if insurance
will cover his second admission in two weeks.

She orders carrot cake, instead,
because it has raisins in every bite
like little jewels strewn on the floor
of a dense forest where there's no trail,

just shadows and tree branches
reaching out, blocking or showing
the way, it's hard to tell which,
so you stumble along and when
you fall to your knees

caught in a thicket because you forgot
to bring a machete into this forest
you might find there something
as useless as a ruby or emerald
which you'll put in your pocket

because it's evidence of magic
and cannot the same be said of a raisin,
sweet on the tongue of a woman
alone at table six in the harsh light
of Frankie's Diner,
half a mile down the road
from the detox center.

Holding the Pin between Her Teeth

She's the woman in silent flicks
tied to the rails, bug-eyed with terror.
Run over by the same train again and again.

Distant whistle she hears
in her sleep becomes a groan,
turns into steps on the landing,
a knock on the bedroom door.
She covers her eyes with her hands,
futile reflex. She's blind in the dark.

She spits coins & cash & checks
at her nightmare
until she's the empty cash drawer
at the boarded-up Citgo.
Screams a string of vowels
until all she has left
are her dictionary lips
in the green of the night.
Into the nightmare's gullet,
she tosses lamps, light bulbs and all,
DVD player, frying pan and leaf blower.

It eats rugs, an aquarium,
everything she shoves at it
to keep it away from her heart,
kept locked in a cage.
Her heart, dyed blue as a bird,
a disguise foolish as moustache and toupee.
Even blue it's still a heart.

Ripped from its cage, it bleeds
red, warm and glistening.
It thumps and thuds in her cupped hands.
She holds it like a sacrifice.

She holds it as it slithers and slides
and surrenders. Viscous as hope,
her bloody heart. It's the only grenade
she has left to throw at the oncoming train.

He Said

he was just tired.
He said he knew nothing
about missing change.
He said he was tired.
He said what's wrong
with long sleeves?
He said he needed money
for gas, food, rent.
He said he needed
to be bailed out.
He said the needles
belong to Randy's brother.
He said he had to pay them back
or they'd kill him.
He said you don't understand
what it's like.
He said rehab. He said no rehab beds.
He said I have sepsis, I have Hep C.
He said I have a bed.
He said they don't know what they're doing,
I'm out of here.
He said bullshit, fuck you, I hate you.
He said I have a detox bed.
He said I just need a ride, no money.
He said I need money. He said I love you.
He said you don't understand,
I'm outside, it's pouring, It's snowing,
I'm freezing, I'll die, I have sun poisoning,
someone stole my phone,
my ID is missing, my face is abscessed,
I'm hungry, I love you. I may
have a job tomorrow, I need money today,
I have cellulitis, you don't understand,
I miss the family, I can't stop.
I need help, there are no beds,

there's a bed, I'll be honest, I used again,
I have kidney failure, you don't understand,
I just need forty, can you make it sixty, fuck you.
I haven't eaten, someone took my coat,
my prescriptions, my cell phone,
I have court tomorrow. I love you.
I need a ride, I'm on the bus,
I'm in the hospital, I'm in jail, I'm under the bridge,
I'll meet you at Sav-A-Lot,
I was kidnapped, I owe them three hundred,
your ring's in the pawn shop, your leaf blower,
lawn mower, laptop's
in the pawn shop, I pawned my car,
tell everyone I love them, miss them,
I hate everyone. Can you bring me food?
It's the 4th of July, my birthday, Thanksgiving,
Christmas, they have a gun to my head.
Can you give me twenty,
forty, eighty, two hundred?
I'm going in tomorrow, I promise,
this is it, I'll never ask again,
can you bring me dry clothes, it rained last night,
forty, sixty, a hundred, I won't ask again.
There's no bed. I need a bed.
Sixty, eighty, all you've got,
I won't ask again.
He said, this is it.
He said, I'm falling fast.
I'm falling hard.

Francesca and Sonia

Nine months on the street.
Until the tow, home was the car
with the blown transmission.
Then the cemetery, all-night
laundromat, bus platform.
Then the kick of a boot
and a move-it-along, so he'd walk,
walk, walk all night long.

Five nights in detox. Luxury
of a mattress, shower and a shave,
clothes from the donation box,
then back to the streets.

Hours later he'd use again.
The sadness of worn-down-
until-they're-paper-thin flip-flops.
No roof between him and the needles
of sleet that weren't on the
weatherman's radar.
Just the cravings.

Two women outside the bodega
on Broad Street where he'd go
to escape the weather, sometimes
just to talk, watch as he's cuffed
and shoved into the back of the cruiser.

Four plastic grocery bags
and a backpack hold everything
he owns now. Francesca and Sonia
take them inside   again.

At Memorial Hospital

She's stuck to a pleather chair there
while he writhes like a bug
on the ER floor by the automatic door.
He moans and screams
like she did when she gave birth.
Was slick with wet then, too,
when they plucked him
out of her, forceps to head.
In her arm she tucked her boy,
gave him love, love.

The ER staff doesn't say much
as he spasms when they cuff
a plastic bracelet to his arm.
She hovers, she's the mother.
Holding up? Say what?

Aide hands her a coffee mug.
He's plugged in, IV's shoved in.
She stands above him.
When she reaches out to him,
her hands fall off,
first one, then the other.
The man who steers a sweeper up the hall
doesn't see them crawling on the floor.
Glub. Glub. Oh, such tough luck.
Now kind of hard to touch,
but how does she let go of?

Spell for Detaching

Gather grandmother's
           pawned rings,

    the leaf blower and laptop,
the broken window,

and a combustible body part.
     Yes, a heart.

       This will build the perfect fire—
seething between smolder

and conflagration
       with tongues of flame

          that lick the air.
When the fire screams

with hunger, feed it his needles,
        his infections, collapsed veins,

headlines, handcuffs,
     hospital bed.

        Feed the flames
his kidney failure, abscesses,

putrid socks,
     the stars he sleeps under.

     Feed that fire
until its heat holds you back

from the flames
      that cry your name.

At the Corner of Broad and Chance

On these sidewalks bent men shoot the shit
and some dope, get through these heat wave days.
Haze covers everything like a wet towel.
Plastic bags, newspapers, crumpled cigarette packs
lie like the dead on a battlefield.

Hartford's hot breath refuses to enter
walk-up apartments above boarded-up bodegas.
Even those lucky enough to have a room
drag chairs outside to catch a breeze.

Charlie, Johnnie and Long Shot wish
their buddy luck in detox,
sure he'll be back in a few days, like always.
Maybe enough time to heal blistered feet.

Sisters, wives, and children are folded
photos in back pockets and backpacks
that cut like broken glass when touched.
There's the fix that fixes everything, except this heat.
At the McDonald's around the corner, yellow arches
glint like gold teeth in a mouth of decay.

This Poem

holds a wound in its cup of bitter coffee.
It can't leave the bullet hole alone.
Inserts a finger until the blood geysers
again, then watches the spectacle
from the bleachers. This poem
asks, *Why is the rain not black as the ink
of its words?* This poem is disappointed
that puppies exist. This poem
wants to fill a filigreed urn
with its own ashes. This poem
shoplifts from the merchant
who only has nice things to say.
This poem can swear in six languages
and talks shit about other poems,
especially ones with soul in them.
If this poem had a face, it would
never shave and its beard
would be the address on the wrong
side of the tracks. If this poem
were a saint, it would be Lawrence,
the martyr, who was grilled on a gridiron
and declared, *I'm done on this side, turn me over.*
This poem wants to talk about heaven
from the point of view of the needle.
When this poem is near its end, it will
pull off the road at the next sunset,
sit in silence until darkness erases
its scrawled lines. This poem can't explain
what it's like to be invisible but can refer
you to the absence of the puddle at the end
of the driveway or to the man nodding off
in the shadow of the alley.

Delivering Thanksgiving Dinner Under the Bridge

Sliced turkey, cranberries, stuffing,
sweet potatoes, string beans,
rolls, pumpkin pie, crammed
into the saved plastic containers
Chinese food comes in, stacked
in paper bags stuffed with plastic
forks, knives, paper plates, cups
and napkins, not crystal, china, silver,
ceramic platters, not table and cloth
and grandmas and uncles, not
centerpieces and seconds, prayers
and babies in highchairs, not who's
getting a promotion, new car, facelift,
not touch football in the yard, Crazy Eights,
scraping plates, soaking pots, naps
on leather couches, warm houses,
not bottom's up or bottom dollar,
not hot showers or bacon and eggs
next morning.

Broken Boy: The Fractured Tale

All the King's horses and all the King's men
are confused when the boy jumps over
the candlestick and his pants catch fire.
*Liar, Liar, pants on fire, his nose is longer
than a telephone wire.*

It's not supposed to happen this way so they eat
curds and whey and split the scene.
The boy comes tumbling after but, no matter,
he's wearing a crown and an irresistible grin.

Soon, he nods off under the haystack,
with the needle; impossible to find. Hey diddle,
diddle, here's a riddle: Where did 9 go?
Didn't you know? 7-8-9!

Well, the boy's eating Christmas pie
in the 'hood. Puts in his thumb
and pulls out a bundle. *A penny for a ball
of thread / Another for a needle*
That's the way the money goes.
How much more can he wheedle?

Then, once upon a time, in the land of Nod,
the dish runs away with the spoon. Soon
the breadcrumb path through the forest
leads to a house covered in candy. He eats

everything until his belly aches.
He begs for a bowl of porridge
or some Tums for his tummy
and a couch to crash on.

He calls the old lady who lives in a shoe;
she'll know what to do. If she doesn't answer
he'll huff and he'll puff.
(*three, four, knock at the door*)

Round and round and round he goes.
How he'll land no one knows.
Ashes, ashes, we all fall down.

The Summer of Fire

A hole in the bucket and the fire
rages. Pillars tall as oaks.
The woman scoops from the lake
until the bucket's filled.
Empty when she reaches the heat.

Spittle kisses flame. The woman
can't stop from trying. The effort
is obsession, denial, penance, pathos.
Even these words burn like leaves.
The way leaves curl into themselves.
The way a body curls into itself
with the kick of a boot.

What's left when words are ash
and the bucket's rusted out,
smolders and broods,
flares into light like the halos
around ancient saints.

Unquenchable, unstoppable light.
Flame flexes muscle.
Tentacles of heat whip and blister
the air. She's not the monk in the square:
she's the fire, she's the bucket.

Christmas Visit

Tomorrow her son returns to his room
at the Y after he's dosed at the clinic.
Tomorrow in his meal-in-a-microwave room,
in his room with no closet.

Everything he owns stacked against walls.
Her son in a room teeming with dreams
packed in boxes and bags stacked
against green or blue or tan walls at the Y.

Her son with the pale face rises from sleep,
reaches for something only he can see.
Colorless shadows thrown by boxes
stacked against walls in a room.
Shadows shifting with the restless light.
Her son dreaming of exits.

Her son is an exit wound big as the moon.
He runs his fingers over the arm he reads
like a book. His needlework like Braille.
Flesh welded shut. Eyes welded shut.
Her son in a box in a box in a box in a box.

Ritual

The hypodermic of despair.
The thrill of blood
blossoming in the soil
of unwashed flesh.

He licks the droplets
as he releases
band from arm.

The bottle cap
in which alchemized
remnants swirl,
he lifts to his lips
like a chalice.

This is his religion.

The acolyte child
performs his ritual
in the back seat
of a car, parked
outside another
detox facility
with a name like

New Hope
Turning Point
First Step
Fresh Start
Better Times Ahead

or *Here We Go Again*.
He heaves his bundle
of belongings onto the bent
spoon of his back, buzzes.
Another metal door
swings open.

One Summer Day

Before the needle shuddered in his arm.
Before the bent spoon, bent back, the strap.
Before complaining veins.
Before a procession of scabs jeweled his flesh.
Before his half-lidded chase for what couldn't be caught.
Before sepsis and Hep C.
Before the trampled path into the woods behind Sav-A-Lot.
Before unforgiving rain, endless snow, blistering heat.
Before donated blankets and gloves, shoplifted sun-block.
Before the cardboard sign held up to passing cars.
Before waiting for someone to toss their cigarette
as they entered a store so he could snatch it,
bring it to his lips and dry hump it back to life.
Before long sleeves in summer and pawn tickets
stashed under football trophies.
Before the oxy parties.
Before the root canal. The script.
The refills.
Before *ashes, ashes, we all fall down.*
There was a boy who loved his skateboard,
how it took him where he wanted to go,
toward all that might have been.

Recovery Prayer

The curtain's parted just enough
so daylight sneaks through. The sun
doesn't need to flood the room just yet.

Like the starving man at the Bottomless Buffet,
take it slow. Otherwise is your thin shadow.
Check the rearview mirror for the 18-wheeler
that travels the rain-slicked road. Take it slow.

Look up except when walking the cusp
of the canyon.

Move forward unless the ice
beneath you begins to crack or the tide
grabs your knees or the flames
reach out for your hand or the grenade
comes rolling, rolling toward you.

Hold onto hope like it's the rope swaying
above raging waters, a hand in the dark,
the ladder outside the burning room, the rail
above the abyss.

Hold on to the homily, the stars
in the matte black night, the photograph
in the wallet, to the poem or song or
blossoming rose, hold on to that splinter
of light, the voice you used to know.

Acknowledgments

Grateful acknowledgment is made to the following publications where these poems or earlier versions of them first appeared:

"He Said" appears in *The Fourth River*, Spring 2019, under the title "A Quiet Storm Gathers."

"Denial" appears in *The Comstock Review*, Spring/Summer 2019.

"The Addict's Mother" appears in *Wingless Dreamer*, Summer 2019.

"One Summer Day" and "Broken Flesh" appear in *Here: a poetry journal*, January 2020.

Praise for
Staring Down the Tracks

From the opening image of a young man "clothespin-thin," lugging "bundles / of belongings down a dirt path," Julia Paul is prepared to stare down reality, no matter how familiar or heartbreaking. Images precise and severe are accompanied by a fragile, defiantly beautiful music as the poet describes the son whom she will lose, over and over again, a boy so spectral that "he leans against a plank of light." As he prepares to enter yet another detox center, her son will heave "his bundle / of belongings onto the bent / spoon of his back." The story is all too familiar; the poems are much more than familiar—brave, articulate, acutely observant.

—Erica Funkhouser, author of *Post & Rail*,
winner of the Idaho Prize for Poetry

Staring Down the Tracks is an extraordinary, elegant collection of poetry about the dire, dreadful, heartbreakingly common experience of opiate addiction and its ravages. If Sylvia Plath were the mother of an addict, she would write poems like "Holding the Pin between Her Teeth," "Spell for Detaching," "The Summer of Fire," and so many others. With nearly 200 people dying every day of overdoses, everyone should read this.

—Miriam Greenspan, psychotherapist and author of
*Healing Through the Dark Emotions:
The Wisdom of Grief, Fear, and Despair.*

Julia Paul's poetry collection *Staring Down the Tracks* takes you inside addiction's silences to reveal, in honed works of lyricism, a mother's relentless worry and pain and grief as her son, who "loved his skateboard," now finds "no vein for happy" and sleeps where "bridge becomes roof." Paul has pulled these words, somehow, from the far reaches of the unsayable. This book will help families engulfed in addiction know that they are not alone and give others insight into its horror. It is a courageous and generous collection, an essential contribution to literature about addiction that will change you.

—Daniel Donaghy, author of *Somerset: Start with the Trouble,* winner of the Paterson Prize for Literary Excellence

About the Author

Julia Paul serves as president of the Riverwood Poetry Series, a longstanding reading series in Hartford, Connecticut. In addition to publication in numerous literary journals, both national and international, including *The Comstock Review, Minerva Rising, New Mexico Review, The Fourth River, Windmill* and *Connecticut Review* and anthologies such as *From Under the Bridges of America, The Heart of All that Is* and *Lavandaria*, several of her poems have been performed in stage productions. Her first book, *Shook*, was published by Grayson Books. Paul served as Manchester, Connecticut's first Poet Laureate, 2014-2019. She is an elder law attorney and the proud mother of three grown sons.

About The Poetry Box®

The Poetry Box® is a boutique publishing company that enjoys providing a platform for both established and emerging poets to share their words with the world through beautiful printed books and chapbooks.

Feel free to visit the online bookstore (thePoetryBox.com), where you'll find more titles including:

November Quilt by Penelope Scambly Schott

Shrinking Bones by Judy K. Mosher

Fireweed by Gurdrun Bortman

Surreal Expulsion by D.R. James

Impossible Ledges by Dianne Avey

Abruptio by Melissa Fournier

Like the O in Hope by Jeanne Julian

What She Was Wearing by Shawn Aveningo Sanders

Moroccan Holiday by Lauren Tivey

Hello, Darling by Christine Higgins

Falling into the River by Debbie Hall

Shadow Man by Margaret Chula

A Long, Wide Stretch of Calm by Melanie Green

and more . . .

www.ingramcontent.com/pod-product-compliance
Lightning Source LLC
LaVergne TN
LVHW020455080526
838202LV00057B/5970